The Proper Windows 10 User Guide
for Beginners & Seniors

master windows 10 setup, tricks, apps & troubleshooting

TREY C. ROLAND

The Proper Windows 10 User Guide

Master windows 10 setup, tricks, apps & troubleshooting

TREY C. ROLAND

Copyright© 2020

Dedicated to readers

Many thanks to Felix Whitehead, my bosom friend, for inspiring me to write tech-related books

Contents

Introduction 9

Windows 10 Setup 10

Step-by-step method for installing Windows 10 11

Windows 10 setup problems 21

Using the Windows Update Troubleshooter 22

Disk space is not enough..24

Errors..27

Hardware incompatible 29

Windows 10 Tips and Tricks...30

Minimize other windows but leave the active one 31

The 'little-known' Start menu 33

Create events without entering the app......................35

Taking a screenshot on the Windows 10 37

Use your keyboard to open taskbar items...................39

Free disk space 41

Stop Start menu ads..43

Block apps from running in the background...............45

Background scrolling...47

See file extensions when you're in File Explorer 49

The improved Game Bar 50

Timeline in Windows 52

Connect phone and PC 54

The Cloud Clipboard on Windows 10 55

Go dark with the Dark mode 57

Use Linux on Windows 59

Sandbox 61

Use Kaomoji on Windows 62

Snip & Sketch 65

Use Nearby Sharing 67

The improved Game Bar 69

Timeline in Windows 71

Connect phone and PC 73

The Cloud Clipboard on Windows 10 74

Go dark with the Dark mode 76

Use Linux on Windows 78

.Sandbox 80

Use Kaomoji on Windows 81

Snip & Sketch 84

Use Nearby Sharing 86

How to Set Up Cortana on Windows 10 88

Setting up Cortana 90

How to set up 'Hey Cortana' 92

Pinning Cortana to the Windows taskbar 94

Train Cortana to recognize your voice 96

Troubleshooting Windows 10 98

Computer is frozen by upgrade 99

Safe mode 100

Recovery console 101

System Restore 102

Printer compatibility 103

Struggling with the touchpad 105

Needless notifications 107

10 Best Windows 10 Apps 109

About The Author 132

Disclaimers 133

Introduction

The title of this book gives a hint on what the book is about. It is a guide for seniors and new users of any of the Windows 10 operating system.

Readers will be introduced into Windows 10 setup with screenshots, tricks, networking basics and troubleshooting. .

Also, readers will learn how to configure and customize Windows 10, manage files and folders, and explore Cortana, Windows 10 voice assistant. .

The last chapter provides insight on the most interesting windows 10 apps.

Now, start savoring the content of this book.

Windows 10 Setup

Upgrading to Windows 10 is a smooth course for some, but for others, not so much. It's a good idea to upgrade to a newer Windows version so that you are able to get security updates and all the cool new features that come with the new version.

But that doesn't mean that the process would be an easy one. Some of the files and that the previous Windows version left behind could cause trouble for the new one. The apps on the system would also be affected.

As a result, many suggest a Clean Install. You must have heard of this term before because it's commonly used. But what it means is that the computer will reformat the hard drive then install the new Windows. All you have to do later is restore your documents and copy your apps back to your PC.

But then, we'll still face a problem. If you are trying to upgrade to Windows 10 from Windows 8 or 7, you can't upgrade through a disc, you will have to download it. And then, you also don't get a product key for your Windows 10 so after you do the Clean Install, you can't activate it. Thankfully, you can get around this issue. These are the steps to take to install Windows 10 on your computer.

Step-by-step method for installing Windows 10

Step 1

Windows

Edition	Windows 10 Pro
Activation	Windows is activated

Change product key

Start by backing up everything on your computer. After that, perform an Upgrade Install rather than a Clean Install. To do a Clean Install, you first need to install the upgrade automatically. When you have done an Upgrade Install, confirm that it's been activated.

1. Go to **Start**
2. Then **Settings**
3. Choose **Update & Security**
4. Select **Activation**

Look for the option that says **Activation: Windows is activated**. If you can't find that confirmation of activation, you will need to give Windows 10 some time to activate first. Until Windows 10 is activated, don't proceed to the next step.

Step 2

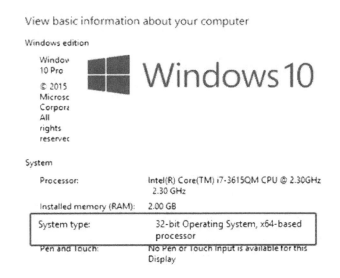

Now, you'll need to find out the Windows 10 version you have. You don't want to download another version. You should find the version of Windows 10 in the **Update & Security** window. To get there

1. Go to **Start**

2. Then **Settings**
3. Choose **Update & Security**
4. Select **Activation**

You should find **Edition:** Windows 10 (version)

Also, find out if you are using a 64 or a 32 bit version. You won't find it in the Update & Security window. Instead, you'll have to go to

1. Go to **Start**
2. Find **Control Panel**
3. Choose **System & Security**
4. Select **System**
5. You'll see if you use a 64 or 32 bit OS from the **System type** section

Step 3

Now, you need to get the Windows 10 Media Creation tool. If you are downloading Windows 10, it should be about 2.5GB. After downloading, copy it to a Flash drive or use an empty DVD to install. Open your browser and enter *microsoft.com/en-gb/software-download/windows10*. Select the button for **Download tool now**.

What this does is that it downloads an undersized setup file that will prompt you to download the other setup tools later.

Step 4

When you have downloaded it, insert your empty DVD or a flash drive. Look in your Downloads folder for the file name; **MediaCreationTool.exe**. Click it twice so that it runs. The setup window should come on. Rather than select **Upgrade this PC**, choose the option for **Create installation media for another PC**. Select **Next**

Step 5

When the next screen comes on, select your Language, Operating System Architecture and Edition. In Architecture, you'll be choosing either 64-bit or 32-bit, make sure it matches your current Windows version. You also don't want to choose the N versions because you don't get Windows Media Player with those.

Step 6

> **What do you want to do?**
>
> ● Upgrade this PC now
> ○ Create installation media for another PC

Choose the device that will be used for Windows 10 installation. If you select **ISO file**, you will be burning the file into your DVD, if you select **USB flash drive**, you will be saving it to your flash drive. Hit **Next**.

Choose the flash drive you want to store the Windows 10 install files and hit **Next** to start the download. If you decided to use a DVD and you selected the ISO file, you will have to burn the file to that disc before you are able to use it for your computer.

Step 7

Start installing Windows 10. Depending on whether you selected USB Flash drive or you burned to DVD select the option for **Install Now** and you'll be prompted to add a product key, select **Skip** and Windows should be activated. It'll be fine without a product key. As long as you have upgraded to Windows 10 earlier and you saw the option for **Activate: Windows is activated** you don't need to add product key

Step 8

> **Upgrade: Install Windows and keep files, settings and applications**
> The files, settings and applications are moved to Windows with this option. This option is only available when a supported version of Windows is already running on the computer.

> **Custom: Install Windows only (advanced)**
> The files, settings and applications aren't moved to Windows with this option. If you want to make changes to partitions and drives, start the computer using the installation disc. We recommend backing up your files before you continue.

You will be asked to select between **Custom Install** where you'll also install Windows without your files or to choose **Upgrade Install** where you'll install Windows 10 but still keep your files. Select **Custom Install** and this will prompt Windows to clear everything on your drive. This is the reason you want to make sure to backup before you even begin Step 1. This way, you can copy your files to the computer after Windows erases everything.

Step 9

Choose the drive partition you would like to install Windows 10. You should see the label Windows 10, or Windows 8 or Windows 7. Whatever Windows version is there, it would be the largest file on the list. If you are still confused about the drive partition to select, find out more before you proceed with the wrong one.

If you are okay with your selection, hit the option for **Format** and **OK** on the pop up box that shows. When it is formatted, choose the option for **Next** to proceed.

Step 10

Finish up Windows 10 setup. Before everything is completed, you will be asked to add a product key for Windows 10 again. Like we said earlier, you don't need to add this, simply hit the option for **Do this later** and continue with the remaining set up options.

Windows 10 setup problems

Just like any other piece of software, Windows 10 is prone to glitches, errors and faults when installing. When this happens, you could easily get confused. In this section, we'll be talking about some of the problems that you could face when you are installing Windows 10 as well as some possible fixes.

Using the Windows Update Troubleshooter

You get a troubleshooter with Windows 10 and it can detect problems automatically. Sometimes, it would even try to fix them. But if the issue isn't obvious and you don't know what to do, you can try using this troubleshooter to identify the problem. To be fair, this wouldn't really help you find a fix but it's better than nothing

1. In the search box, enter **Troubleshoot**. From the options that show, choose **Troubleshoot**.
2. You will find a window for Troubleshoot. Look in the section entitled **Get up and running** and select the **Windows Update**.
3. When you click Windows Update, you should see the **Run the Troubleshooter**

button. Choose this button to run the troubleshooter automatically

4. This will open a troubleshooter window to scan for any Windows 10 problems. It will search for corrupted files and for missing tools and if any issue is found, you will be notified. You will then be prompted to select either Skip This Fix or Apply This Fix. If you want a solution to your problem, simply select **Apply This Fix**. If you know what to do and only needed the troubleshooter to identify the problem for you, select **Skip This Fix**

5. When it is done, you will see the problems that are fixed and you can end it by hitting **Close**. If issues weren't found, then the next option is to update again.

Disk space is not enough

When installing Windows 10, you need to have space on your hard disk to start the installation process. If you are using a lower laptop or a tablet, you will be installing the 32-bit operating system and that requires about 16GB of space. You will need to have 20GB free space if you are installing the 64-bit version of the OS.

If you are using the Microsoft Upgrade Tool to install the file from your system, be sure to have an extra 4GB free space for the files needed for installation. To ensure that you have enough space for installation, the OS will also keep about 7GB space available.

So if you've got a storage drive, you will want to make sure that you clear some things and make room for the installation. The fastest way to do this to get rid of the apps that take the most space. This will mean letting go of your 3D games that are like a billion GB and other complex programs. You can backup your files so that you can get your settings and information back. If you back up, you can re-install your apps when you have Windows 10 up and running.

If you find that you still need more space for Windows 10, the next thing to attack is your Video files, then your Audio files. Next to audio you have your Image files. If you see anything you really don't wish to delete, simply save it to an external USB hard drive. It will also be super easy to get your files back when everything's worked out

Even after deleting, get into the Recycle Bin and clear out the files you just deleted for good. You can also get apps to help you get rid of storage space eaters like browser caches and others. A good example is **CCleaner**. You can check for the amount of space left by

1. Entering **Start**
2. Search for **This PC** and select it
3. To continue with the installation, ensure you have at least 20GB. Windows 10 will install in the Windows drive.

Errors

While setting up Windows 10, you could see an error code at some point in the installation process. There are a gazillion error codes that could show up and each has their different fixes. Your best choice at finding a solution is to write the code on a piece of paper then paste it into Google and see if anyone has put up a solution for that code. Techy forums are a great way to start.

If you don't find anything helpful, you can try these measures for a start
1. Disconnect external devices like keyboards, flash drives, monitors and other kinds of dongles or drives. If you connected the power cord, leave that in. If there's anything your computer needs, it's extra power.
2. If you use a Desktop computer, you will want to remove other internal hardware. If

a sound or graphics card comes integrated with the motherboard, get rid of individual cards. USB extensions, fan controllers, card readers, disc drive should also be disconnected.

3. If you chose a standard upgrade while upgrading to Windows 10, you will want to get rid of unuseful programs. Device drivers and Anti-Viruses tend to be a pain while installing Windows 10

4. Try doing a Clean Install. Back up your precious file and rather than **Upgrade** just choose **Custom: Install Windows**

Hardware incompatible

There are different hardware that Windows 10 runs on and even though it should be compatible with many computers, the OS has its minimum requirements. If you use the 32-bit version, you will want to make sure that you have at least 1GB RAM. For the 64-bit version, 2GB is that minimum.

The PC's processor should also be at least 1GHz. If you don't have these, you will not be allowed to finish the setup process. If you use Desktop, it shouldn't be that hard to get a faster processor and to up the RAM. Laptop users, on the other hand, will have it hard this time.

Windows 10 Tips and Tricks

It doesn't matter whether you are a new user or you've been with Windows 10 for a long time, you will need to learn some shortcuts and tricks to speed up your work. Being productive means being able to shut down apps and start processes in the blink of an eye.

The hidden features aren't in some kind of Microsoft manual and this can make it harder to discover them and make the most out of your computer. But in this guide, we'll be discussing some tricks to help you get more done with your Windows 10 PC.

Minimize other windows but leave the active one

You would think it wouldn't exist but there's actually a trick to minimize all windows without closing the active one. Yes, you can easily enter each window and close them yourself one by one but where's the fun in that? Besides not begin efficient, it's a really slow process and you would understand how vital this shortcut is when you have about 9 windows open at once.

All you have to do to make this work is
1. Enter the window you want to stay open.
2. Click the title bar of that window. If you don't know what the title bar is it's the very top area of any window you enter.

3. Hold down on this title bar and shake it back and forth.

It shouldn't be long before the other windows are minimized after some shakes. With this, the only window that will remain open is the window you shook.

This is very useful if you've opened a series of programs only to see that the desktop screen is crowded and full of windows from different apps. If you don't want to take the time to minimize them one by one, you can just use this efficient trick.

The 'little-known' Start menu

It is not that popular and you may never have heard about it before, but there's a hidden Start menu in the Start button. You haven't discovered it yet not because you have to turn something on in the settings but because you haven't stumbled on it,

It's kind of hidden in plain sight but when you access it, you will be able to reach the Control Panel, Command Prompt and Task Manager. It's very easy to reach this menu. All you need to do is reach the Start menu/Windows Button at the bottom left corner of the screen and instead of clicking, right click.

What you'll get is a list of admin tools as also quick shortcuts for shutting down. If you want to view the desktop quickly, you also get a Desktop link.

The process is quite different, though, if you are using a touchscreen computer.

What you'll do instead is press and hold this Start menu/Windows Button and it will be opened to you. There's also a keyboard shortcut to reach this menu; it's **Windows Key + X**. This will allow you to see shortcuts and tools that will normally take you ages to find. If you wanted to find the Command Prompt, you will have to enter the **All apps** section then find **Windows systems**. But with this hidden Start menu, it's right there on the list.

Create events without entering the app

There's an in-built calendar app in Windows 10 but you don't always have to enter the app to use its features. You can create events and view them using the taskbar on the screen. If you want, you could even connect your iCloud or Google Calendar and see what you have planned for the day right from the taskbar.

If you want to use the calendar without entering the app, you will have to use the clock on the taskbar. You can select the option for **Show Agenda** if events don't show up. Hit the **Hide Agenda** option if you want to conceal your events.

If you add any event to the calendar app, it will show up on the taskbar. And also if you add any event to the taskbar it will show up on the calendar app. You can still use some core features of the calendar right from the taskbar. To add an event;

1. Select the time and date box on your taskbar
2. Select the date you want to plan an event
3. Add the time, date and location for the event.
4. Hit the **Save** option and the event will show up in the calendar. If you have linked your Google Calendar, it will also show up across all connected devices.

Taking a screenshot on the Windows 10

Yeah, you might be thinking it's a simple one but a lot of people don't know how to take screenshots on their computer. We use our phones a lot so taking a screenshot only needs a gesture at least a few buttons. But when it comes to computers, we basically forget the process.

And the funny thing is that they are countless methods of taking a screenshot on your computer and Windows 10 also opens even more possibilities.

For starters, you can capture your entire screen very quickly by pressing the **Print Screen Key + Windows Key** combo. You should find the screenshot in the Pictures folder, then Screenshots But what if you only wanted to capture a small section of the screen? Print Screen wouldn't cut it.

You will have to use the Snipping Tool. Simply select the Windows Key and search for **Snipping Tool**. This will open up the Snipping Tool window. Press **New** to capture a little area of the screen.

Use your keyboard to open taskbar items

Keyboard shortcuts are the fastest way to navigate the system and with each OS version, you get even more shortcuts to make things efficient. If you pinned apps on your taskbar, they'll automatically be given a number. After the Start menu/Windows Button, the next app is the first, No. 1, the next is No. 2 and it goes all the way to 9. For the tenth app, it will be No. 0.

The reason you want to know these numbers is that they are needed for this shortcut. If you want to launch the first app with your keyboard, simply press down the **Windows Key + 1** and the app will open up.

To open up the fifth app on the taskbar, press **Windows Key + 5**. You should get the picture now. You want to click the Windows Key together with the number that's equivalent to the app's position on the taskbar. If you want to launch the tenth app, trying **Windows Key + 10** wouldn't work. It will be **Windows Key + 0** instead. Pretty neat, right?

Free disk space

Do you want to free up some space on your computer? There's a screen made on Windows 10 for that sole purpose. With this, you can see how much room you have left and what is taking the most space. You also get the Storage Sense feature that gives you the chance to get rid of items in the Recycle Bin and temporary files.

The storage screen on Windows 10 updates has been refurbished to make viewing easier. With this, you can easily find out the tools you have available for freeing your hard disk of junk. If you don't have the updated version, enter the **Update & Security** section in the **Settings** to upgrade your OS.

You can find out about your storage when you

1. Enter the **Settings**
2. Then **System**
3. Select **Storage**.

From here, you can see the space available as well as how much has been used up already. You also get to see data broken down into different segments. At the top of the page, you get Storage Sense. You can configure this feature by choosing the opting for **Configure Storage Sense.** From here, you can select when downloads and temporary files can be removed as well as how many times you want the tool to run.

Stop Start menu ads

So you got your Windows 10 for free and that's amazing. But Windows makes up for this with a masked section for ads. This will lead you to buy services and applications you really don't want. But the thing is that whether you got your Windows 10 with your new computer, you paid for the Windows 10 Pro or you upgraded for free, the ads will show up almost everywhere

Some view these ads as a way to find out more about what their Windows 10 can offer but for others, it simply just affects how they work with their computer and it can be pretty annoying. As long as you know where to go and which button to toggle, Windows 10 gives you the ability to cancel these ads.

One reason you haven't found the turn off button for the ads on the Start menu is probably that you are looking for 'Ads'. You won't find it. Microsoft calls it Suggested.

- ❖ Enter the **Settings**
- ❖ Choose **Personalization**
- ❖ Select **Start**
- ❖ Disable the option for **Occasionally Show Suggestions In Start**

If you are also looking to remove these ads from your lock screen,

- ❖ Get to the **Settings**
- ❖ Select **Personalization**
- ❖ Then **Lock Screen**
- ❖ Find the section for **Background** and click the dropdown menu.
- ❖ Select **Picture**
- ❖ Find the option that says **Get Fun Facts, Tips and More from Windows**……….. Turn off the switch,

Block apps from running in the background

Many apps you get from the Microsoft Store will still run in the background on Windows 10. The reason they run in the background is to use some extra features like sending notifications, downloading information and keeping Live Tiles up to date.

These features are helpful in some cases but most of the time, they'll be a nuisance. They can deplete the battery and squander system resources. If you don't mind your apps not being updated regularly, you can use a Windows 10 feature for controlling what runs in the background.

1. Slide into the **Settings**
2. Select **Privacy**
3. Choose **Background Apps**

4. Find the section entitled; **Choose Which Apps Can Run….**, switch off any app you don't want to be in the background

With this, the apps will be terminated when you close them. Before they can run again, you'll have to open the app again.

Background scrolling

You can scroll on any window on Windows 10 in any direction. You can do that in any Windows version but what makes Windows 10 unique is that you don't need to be working on the app to scroll on it. If you have many windows open and you want to look through them, this would prove useful.

To use this feature, start by launching 2 apps like Microsoft Word and Notepad. Place both apps on the screen so that you can see a glimpse of one app with its texts. While you are working on Notepad, move your mouse to the Microsoft Word window and scroll on it.

Even though you are not working on Microsoft Word and it's not active, you will still be able to scroll. But this cool option isn't available for automatically, you will have to enable it

1. Enter the **Settings**
2. Then **Devices**
3. Choose **Mouse**
4. Enable the option for **Scroll Inactive Windows When I Hover….**

See file extensions when you're in File Explorer

Microsoft doesn't show you file exertions and this can make it hard for those who want to find files by their formats. This is how you make file extensions visible on Windows 10

At the bottom of the screen, type in **File Explorer Options** in the search bar

Enter the **View** tab on the window that opens up

Find the option that says **Hide Extensions For Known File Types** and untick the box.

Choose **Apply** and confirm. With this, you should be seeing file extensions when you enter File Explorer.

There are other things you can turn on with **File Explorer Options** so look around and enable what suits you.

The improved Game Bar

You can summon the Game Bar when you hit the **Windows Key + G** combo and if you love playing around with your computer, you'll be happy to know that this section holds a lot of fun features. You can record clips of gameplay, take a screenshot or record a video.

With the combination of the fascinating Game Mode option with game streaming, you get a lot of essential options. With the new updates, you also get features you don't see anywhere else. You get an interface you can customize easily. With this new interface, you get an audio widget, an interface like Discord, a performance widget, integration with Spotify as well as Xbox Live friends interface.

These are top features anyone would love to have and newer updates even give you the ability to monitor GPU temperature and more. Even if you don't play yourself, you could see use the Game Bar's features to record videos from just about any app on your PC.

In Windows 10's Start menu, you get a separate category to fiddle with some settings like parental controls and Xbox networking.

Timeline in Windows

With Timeline on your Windows 10 PC, you will be able to continue work from where you left off. All you have to do is select the button for Task View that's shown on the taskbar. You can also summon the feature by hitting **Windows Key + Tab**.

As the name suggests, this will show you a timeline of your applications. You can see how much you've used certain apps in the past. A more useful feature is the option to categorize relevant apps into a particular group in your timeline.

With this, when you launch that budget document, the sites and tasks that were linked when you were using it will be triggered too. You could also get this setting to sync across devices so if you have several computers, you can use it to keep track on your other systems

It's a pretty handy feature but this is where things get dicey. Not all apps are compatible with this Timeline feature. But that there are tools from Microsoft that allow app developers to make their apps compatible with Timeline. And the worst part is that Microsoft Edge is the only browser that supports Timeline. If you don't want to use Timeline, you can deactivate it.

1. Enter the **Settings**
2. Choose **Privacy**
3. Select **Activity History**

Connect phone and PC

Would you like to link up your computer and smartphone together? You can simply use the Your Phone application on the Windows 10 OS to view the photos you recently shot with your mobile device. If you are in the mood for some messages, you could even send SMS, get notifications from the phone, make a call, work with the apps on your phone and see your device's battery life

To make this work, you will have to get the Your Phone app from the Google Play Store on your smartphone. If you use an iPhone, you can get the Your Phone app for iOS also but not all features are available to iPhone users.

The Cloud Clipboard on Windows 10

Over the years, the copy and paste function of Windows 10 hasn't been a smooth ride but it seems things are looking up now. You can use Cloud Clipboard to sync texts across different computers. This is a really helpful feature that was brought in 2018. If you would like to turn on this clipboard feature,

1. Enter the **Start**
2. Choose **Settings**
3. Then **System**
4. Select **Clipboard**
5. Turn on the option for **Sync Across Devices**.

What this will do is that it'll give you the opportunity to transfer data from one computer to the other. If you want to take things further, enable the option for Clipboard History so that you will be able to save texts and other important information on your clipboard and paste them when you need to.

If you want to use this feature, you can fire up Cloud Clipboard window by pressing **Windows Key + V** and you should see the menu. All devices signed in on the same Microsoft account will be able to access this clipboard history. Click on the texts you would like to copy and use the traditional **Ctrl + V** to paste what you just copied.

Go dark with the Dark mode

Everyone loves Dark themes. For one thing, we've all been stuck with the default light themes for decades so we'll jump on any chance to try something new. Then there's the perk of it being easy on the eyes. Light themes are great for daytime and bright light environments but when you are in the dark or at night, they can scorch your eyes.

So when the bright light from the computer gets too bright and you need to tone it down a little, you can easily switch to the Dark version of windows.

1. Get to the **Start menu**
2. Select **Settings**
3. Then **Personalization**
4. Select **Color**

5. In the section for **Choose Your Default App Mode**, select **Dark**.

Use Linux on Windows

Thanks to the collaboration of Microsoft and Canonical, Linux on Windows is now a thing. It was unbelievable to hear that Bash Shell would arrive on Windows. If you don't know what Bash on Windows means, it gives a subsystem where Linux is able to run. Don't think of it as a virtual app or machine, it's a real Linux system on Windows.

You'll be able to use the original Bash Shell that Linux makes available to users on Windows. There are many other ways to get Linux on Windows

The first method is to go through PowerShell. To get to PowerShell on your Windows 10 pc,
1. Enter the **Start menu**
2. Type in **PowerShell** and you'll see Windows PowerShell appear.
3. Right click on it and select **Run as Administrator**

You can also try using virtual machines. With these machines, you will be able to use any OS on your computer. You can use VMware Player or VirtualBox for this. All you then have to do is install Ubuntu in that virtual machine the same way would install it on a normal computer

If you ever need to boot the Linux system, you use a window on the desktop for it. You don't have to leave your programs on Windows.

Another way to get Linux on Windows is by using Cygwin. Cygwin gives you different tools that offer you an environment like Linux but you'll be doing it on Windows.

Sandbox

With Windows Sandbox, you will be able to use unknown websites or apps in a safe environment. What happens is that Sandbox provides a duplicated version of Windows where you will be able to open apps and processes you don't trust.

If your sixth sense was right and things go south, the duplicated virtual version simply goes off and comes back on. If nothing bad happens and the task works normally, you can welcome it into your original Windows 10.

It's a great way to keep your system safe from threats but there's a little snag; only those with Windows 10 Pro are able to use Windows Sandbox.

Use Kaomoji on Windows

So everyone knows about Emojis and it's been trending over the last couple of years but let's drop that. The new update to Windows 10 now gives you features like Kaomoji. With this, you will be able to use some shortcuts on your keyboard to choose Emoji-like lettering.

Kaomojis aren't really popular around the world but in Japan, they are the bomb. Emojis are images, quite all right, but Kaomojis are emoticons based on texts. You just have to find the Emoji picker on Windows 10 to use this feature

When you are in any program, hit the **Windows Key + .** (period). If you would like to view your collection of Kaomojis, select the **;-)** button at the upper part of the list. If you can't find this button on this menu, it means you have to update your Windows 10 version.

At the bottom of the list, you can go through different Kaomoji categories using the icons shown. You can also scroll with your mouse to see more Kaomojis. If you don't have a mouse, click the scroll bar on the right and drag it down.

On the main tab, you get the Kaomojis you've used recently which is a great way to easily pick Kaomojis you use regularly. Unfortunately, you'll only be able to use this to see your frequently used Kaomojis as there's not a way to pin favorites.

You can also choose to use only your keyboard to find your way through the interface.
1. Start with the **Windows + .** shortcut to open the interface (remember, that's a period)
2. To choose the icons shown on top, double click **Tab**.
3. To choose a Kaomoji, use the right arrow key and hit **Enter** to trigger it.

4. If you want to change the focus to the Kaomoji library, hit **Tab** and select an icon with your arrow key

Just like that, you can insert a Kaomoji with only the keyboard. If you don't want to add Emojis to a document, using Kaomojis is a great replacement. With each update, Microsoft continues to enrich this collection of Kaomojis.

Snip & Sketch

The Snipping Tool has been made available on Windows for ages, you could easily use this to take screenshots but on a not-so-recent update, a new tool for screenshot was released; Snip & Sketch. With this tool, you will be able to take a screenshot of the whole screen and also the rectangular segment of the screen.

The Snipping Tool could do all that but this is where things get interesting with Snip & Sketch. You can also take a screenshot of a freeform area or set it through a timer so that it isn't taken right away. If you would like to do some mild editing like cropping, this feature also gives you the option for that. You can also highlight and make a drawing on the screenshot.

There are different ways to get to the Snip & Sketch menu

The first method will have you go through the Start menu

- Simply enter the **Start Menu**
- Move through the list of **Apps**
- Choose **Snip & Sketch**

A quicker method of reaching Snip & Sketch is to use the Action Center

- Hit the **Action Center** icon
- Choose the **Screen Snip** action
- You can also use a keyboard key to fire up Snip & Sketch
- Fire up **Settings**
- Choose **Ease Of Access**
- Select the **Keyboard Settings**
- Move down and enable the option for using the Print Screen button for screen snipping

You can also hit the search and type in **Snip & Sketch**

Use Nearby Sharing

With Nearby Sharing, you are able to share files with PCs easily through the air. So you don't need to use chat apps or flash drives to send things to your friends near you. When you fire up the Share menu in File Explorer or Edge, you will be able to view the computers that have turned on Nearby Sharing. You will only be able to see this as an option if you have installed the April 2018 update.

When something has been sent to their computer, the receiver will get a notification. If you use iOS devices, you will know the Apple version as AirDrop. But you don't get support for mobile with Nearby Sharing which is a bummer.

You also need to have a computer with Wi-Fi and Bluetooth. After that, get to the Settings and turn on the option for Nearby Sharing. You don't get a blink-of-an-eye transfer speed and you can pretty much compare it to transferring with Bluetooth. So if you want to transfer heavy files, you'll still need to use drives.

The improved Game Bar

You can summon the Game Bar when you hit the **Windows Key + G** combo and if you love playing around with your computer, you'll be happy to know that this section holds a lot of fun features. You can record clips of gameplay, take a screenshot or record a video.

With the combination of the fascinating Game Mode option with game streaming, you get a lot of essential options. With the new updates, you also get features you don't see anywhere else. You get an interface you can customize easily. With this new interface, you get an audio widget, an interface like Discord, a performance widget, integration with Spotify as well as Xbox Live friends interface.

These are top features anyone would love to have and newer updates even give you the ability to monitor GPU temperature and more. Even if you don't play yourself, you could see use the Game Bar's features to record videos from just about any app on your PC.

In Windows 10's Start menu, you get a separate category to fiddle with some settings like parental controls and Xbox networking.

Timeline in Windows

With Timeline on your Windows 10 PC, you will be able to continue work from where you left off. All you have to do is select the button for Task View that's shown on the taskbar. You can also summon the feature by hitting **Windows Key + Tab**.

As the name suggests, this will show you a timeline of your applications. You can see how much you've used certain apps in the past. A more useful feature is the option to categorize relevant apps into a particular group in your timeline.

With this, when you launch that budget document, the sites and tasks that were linked when you were using it will be triggered too. You could also get this setting to sync across devices so if you have several computers, you can use it to keep track on your other systems

It's a pretty handy feature but this is where things get dicey. Not all apps are compatible with this Timeline feature. But that there are tools from Microsoft that allow app developers to make their apps compatible with Timeline. And the worst part is that Microsoft Edge is the only browser that supports Timeline. If you don't want to use Timeline, you can deactivate it.

1. Enter the **Settings**
2. Choose **Privacy**
3. Select **Activity History**

Connect phone and PC

Would you like to link up your computer and smartphone together? You can simply use the Your Phone application on the Windows 10 OS to view the photos you recently shot with your mobile device. If you are in the mood for some messages, you could even send SMS, get notifications from the phone, make a call, work with the apps on your phone and see your device's battery life

To make this work, you will have to get the Your Phone app from the Google Play Store on your smartphone. If you use an iPhone, you can get the Your Phone app for iOS also but not all features are available to iPhone users.

The Cloud Clipboard on Windows 10

Over the years, the copy and paste function of Windows 10 hasn't been a smooth ride but it seems things are looking up now. You can use Cloud Clipboard to sync texts across different computers. This is a really helpful feature that was brought in 2018. If you would like to turn on this clipboard feature,

1. Enter the **Start**
2. Choose **Settings**
3. Then **System**
4. Select **Clipboard**
5. Turn on the option for **Sync Across Devices**.

What this will do is that it'll give you the opportunity to transfer data from one computer to the other. If you want to take things further, enable the option for Clipboard History so that you will be able to save texts and other important information on your clipboard and paste them when you need to.

If you want to use this feature, you can fire up Cloud Clipboard window by pressing **Windows Key + V** and you should see the menu. All devices signed in on the same Microsoft account will be able to access this clipboard history. Click on the texts you would like to copy and use the traditional **Ctrl + V** to paste what you just copied.

Go dark with the Dark mode

Everyone loves Dark themes. For one thing, we've all been stuck with the default light themes for decades so we'll jump on any chance to try something new. Then there's the perk of it being easy on the eyes. Light themes are great for daytime and bright light environments but when you are in the dark or at night, they can scorch your eyes.

So when the bright light from the computer gets too bright and you need to tone it down a little, you can easily switch to the Dark version of windows.

1. Get to the **Start menu**
2. Select **Settings**
3. Then **Personalization**
4. Select **Color**

5. In the section for **Choose Your Default App Mode**, select **Dark**.

Use Linux on Windows

Thanks to the collaboration of Microsoft and Canonical, Linux on Windows is now a thing. It was unbelievable to hear that Bash Shell would arrive on Windows. If you don't know what Bash on Windows means, it gives a subsystem where Linux is able to run. Don't think of it as a virtual app or machine, it's a real Linux system on Windows.

You'll be able to use the original Bash Shell that Linux makes available to users on Windows. There are many other ways to get Linux on Windows

The first method is to go through PowerShell. To get to PowerShell on your Windows 10 pc,
1. Enter the **Start menu**
2. Type in **PowerShell** and you'll see Windows PowerShell appear.
3. Right click on it and select **Run as Administrator**

You can also try using virtual machines. With these machines, you will be able to use any OS on your computer. You can use VMware Player or VirtualBox for this. All you then have to do is install Ubuntu in that virtual machine the same way would install it on a normal computer

If you ever need to boot the Linux system, you use a window on the desktop for it. You don't have to leave your programs on Windows.

Another way to get Linux on Windows is by using Cygwin. Cygwin gives you different tools that offer you an environment like Linux but you'll be doing it on Windows.

.Sandbox

With Windows Sandbox, you will be able to use unknown websites or apps in a safe environment. What happens is that Sandbox provides a duplicated version of Windows where you will be able to open apps and processes you don't trust.

If your sixth sense was right and things go south, the duplicated virtual version simply goes off and comes back on. If nothing bad happens and the task works normally, you can welcome it into your original Windows 10.

It's a great way to keep your system safe from threats but there's a little snag; only those with Windows 10 Pro are able to use Windows Sandbox.

Use Kaomoji on Windows

So everyone knows about Emojis and it's been trending over the last couple of years but let's drop that. The new update to Windows 10 now gives you features like Kaomoji. With this, you will be able to use some shortcuts on your keyboard to choose Emoji-like lettering.

Kaomojis aren't really popular around the world but in Japan, they are the bomb. Emojis are images, quite all right, but Kaomojis are emoticons based on texts. You just have to find the Emoji picker on Windows 10 to use this feature

When you are in any program, hit the **Windows Key + .** (period). If you would like to view your collection of Kaomojis, select the **;-)** button at the upper part of the list. If you can't find this button on this menu, it means you have to update your Windows 10 version.

At the bottom of the list, you can go through different Kaomoji categories using the icons shown. You can also scroll with your mouse to see more Kaomojis. If you don't have a mouse, click the scroll bar on the right and drag it down.

On the main tab, you get the Kaomojis you've used recently which is a great way to easily pick Kaomojis you use regularly. Unfortunately, you'll only be able to use this to see your frequently used Kaomojis as there's not a way to pin favorites.

- You can also choose to use only your keyboard to find your way through the interface.
- Start with the **Windows + .** shortcut to open the interface (remember, that's a period)
- To choose the icons shown on top, double click **Tab**.

- ❖ To choose a Kaomoji, use the right arrow key and hit **Enter** to trigger it.
- ❖ If you want to change the focus to the Kaomoji library, hit **Tab** and select an icon with your arrow key

Just like that, you can insert a Kaomoji with only the keyboard. If you don't want to add Emojis to a document, using Kaomojis is a great replacement. With each update, Microsoft continues to enrich this collection of Kaomojis.

Snip & Sketch

The Snipping Tool has been made available on Windows for ages, you could easily use this to take screenshots but on a not-so-recent update, a new tool for screenshot was released; Snip & Sketch. With this tool, you will be able to take a screenshot of the whole screen and also the rectangular segment of the screen.

The Snipping Tool could do all that but this is where things get interesting with Snip & Sketch. You can also take a screenshot of a freeform area or set it through a timer so that it isn't taken right away. If you would like to do some mild editing like cropping, this feature also gives you the option for that. You can also highlight and make a drawing on the screenshot.

There are different ways to get to the Snip & Sketch menu

The first method will have you go through the Start menu

1. Simply enter the **Start Menu**
2. Move through the list of **Apps**
3. Choose **Snip & Sketch**
4. A quicker method of reaching Snip & Sketch is to use the Action Center
5. Hit the **Action Center** icon
6. Choose the **Screen Snip** action
7. You can also use a keyboard key to fire up Snip & Sketch
8. Fire up **Settings**
9. Choose **Ease Of Access**
10. Select the **Keyboard Settings**
11. Move down and enable the option for using the Print Screen button for screen snipping
12. You can also hit the search and type in **Snip & Sketch**

Use Nearby Sharing

With Nearby Sharing, you are able to share files with PCs easily through the air. So you don't need to use chat apps or flash drives to send things to your friends near you. When you fire up the Share menu in File Explorer or Edge, you will be able to view the computers that have turned on Nearby Sharing. You will only be able to see this as an option if you have installed the April 2018 update.

When something has been sent to their computer, the receiver will get a notification. If you use iOS devices, you will know the Apple version as AirDrop. But you don't get support for mobile with Nearby Sharing which is a bummer.

You also need to have a computer with Wi-Fi and Bluetooth. After that, get to the Settings and turn on the option for Nearby Sharing. You don't get a blink-of-an-eye transfer speed and you can pretty much compare it to transferring with Bluetooth. So if you want to transfer heavy files, you'll still need to use drives.

How to Set Up Cortana on Windows 10

There are many digital assistants available nowadays and Microsoft's Cortana happens to be one of them. Depending on how you set things up, she would answer when you say her name and be at your beck and call. She can also give you a hand when you are trying to find your way around Windows 10.

Want to know what the weather tomorrow would be like? Ask Cortana. Want to be reminded about an important event coming up soon? Ask Cortana. Cortana is not enabled on Windows 10 by default so you'll have to do the digging yourself and set her up. In this guide, we'll be talking about the steps you need to take to get Cortana up and running

Setting up Cortana

You can easily access Cortana from the taskbar of your computer. You'll have to open the assistant before you can reach the home screen

Select the **Start menu**. If you don't know what this is, it's the Windows icon at the very bottom left corner on every screen.

Select the option for **All Apps**

Choose **Cortana**

Hit the Cortana button just on top of the icon for Windows

Select the option for **Use Cortana**

If you would like to use **Speed, Inking and Typing Personalization**, choose the **Yes** option for that selection. With this, Cortana would be able to know more about you and this would help the assistant complete the tasks you assign her. You can select the **No Thanks** option if you would prefer this option turned off

Now that you have Cortana all set up, you can use her right away. If you want to use the assistant, you can start by typing in your request in the search bar at the bottom and see as she carries it out. But there's a faster way to call up Cortana and it's through 'Hey Cortana'

How to set up 'Hey Cortana'

With 'Hey Cortana', you'll be able to use Cortana without even clicking anything on your computer. With this, you can be away from your PC and summon Cortana with your voice. It's also a great way to multitask.

If you wouldn't like to login on your computer but would still like to use Cortana's services, you can use 'Hey Cortana' to interact with the assistant while you are at the lock screen of your computer.

To enable 'Hey Cortana', hit the search bar present in the taskbar. The window should show up and you'll be able to select the **Notebook** symbol among the options at the left part of the menu

Select the **Settings** icon when the Notebook menu opens up. If you click the Settings before you click the Notebook icon, what you'll get is System Settings rather than Cortana Settings. So the order of selection is crucial

This will then open Cortana Setting. Look for the **'Hey Cortana'** subheading and turn on the option.

With this, you could be using your computer normally and when you need to use Cortana all you have to do is say 'Hey Cortana, do this and this for me' if you are one who uses Cortana on a regular basis, you would find this feature really useful.

You can ask Cortana to do a couple of things for you. When you say "'Hey Cortana'" you can then;
- Tell Cortana to add an item to your grocery list
- Tell Cortana to help you set a reminder at a particular time and date

- Tell Cortana to read what's on your schedule for the day or the next task to be done
- Tell Cortana to find services near you like the closest restaurant or store.
- Tell Cortana to help you with really anything you would like.
- You can also turn on the option for **Use Cortana While Device Is Locked** so that you will be able to summon Cortana even while you're on the lock screen

Pinning Cortana to the Windows taskbar

While it is true that the taskbar is Cortana's home, you won't find her there by default, you'll have to set that up in the Settings. If you don't put Cortana in the taskbar, you'll have to open the app anytime you need her services. If that's a long process for you and would love to save 5 seconds from the process, this is how to pin the assistant to the taskbar

On your Windows 10 taskbar, right click on an empty space
Choose the option for **Cortana**
You will be shown 3 options for how you want Cortana to appear, select your preferred one
Hidden: If you select this option, Cortana would be hidden from the taskbar
Show Cortana icon: If you choose this option, you will be shown Cortana icon on the taskbar
Show Search box: With this, you'll be able to access Cortana via the search bar at the bottom of your screen

Train Cortana to recognize your voice

Microsoft's Cortana works just fine and doesn't need any kind of training or schooling to get her to work well. But if would like to get the assistant's undivided attention, it's a good idea to train her to recognize your voice. With this, you will also get better results when you try to ask her things

Fire up **Cortana**. You can launch Cortana easily from the search bar on the taskbar. You can also enter **All Apps** and choose **Cortana** from the list

This should bring you into the Cortana window. Choose the **Notebook** icon just below the home icon at the left part of the menu

The Notebook menu would open. Select the **Settings** option and check to make sure that you have turned on **'Hey Cortana'**. Just below that option is the option for **Respond Best**. It would automatically be set to **To Anyone**

Select the option for **To Me**. Just below that, select the **Learn My Voice** option. Follow the on-screen directions to register your voice with Cortana.

When that's complete the assistant will understand you even more and will respond faster when you call on her.

Troubleshooting Windows 10

When it comes to popularity, Windows 10 has now surpassed Windows 7 and it's getting bigger with every update. The new OS has been available for about 5 years now and this is ample time for users to know their way around.

Every operating system will present its problems and over the last couple of years since its release, Microsoft has been launching fixes to some of Windows 10 common problems. Nevertheless, there are still some bugs and malfunctions that the update to Windows 10 can cause.

If you are having hard with Windows 10, in this section, we'll be discussing some of the most common problems that you ma fayce on your PC with the new operating system.

Computer is frozen by upgrade

One problem with Windows 10 is that the operating system simply becomes frozen on PCs where it is kept on the SSD. Microsoft has already admitted that this is a flaw, though they also mentioned that they didn't know the cause.

Recently, we have some official recommendations from Microsoft on how users can avoid this freezing. One of the guides was for users of the newer version of Windows 10 to downgrade to an old version without the bug. You can downgrade to an old Windows 10 version and use Windows without hanging.

You can go back to the old version if it still within 10 days of the original upgrade. If you are not able to uninstall the Update through logging in, you can then try these 2 methods

Safe mode

You will have to restart your computer. When you are on the screen for logging in, press and hold the **Shift** key as you hit **Power** then **Restart**

The PC should turn off and turn on again but you will be shown the screen for **Choose an option**.

- Select **Troubleshoot**
- Then **Advanced Options**
- Select **Startup Settings**
- Hit **Restart**

To start your PC in safe mode you can either select F4 or 4.

- Launch the **Settings** app
- Choose **Update & Security** and select the tab for **Recovery**
- Find the **Go back to earlier build** option and hit the button for **Get Started**. Go through with the instructions shown on the screen

Recovery console

1. Start by restarting your computer. When you are shown the sign in page, press and hold the **Shift** key as you hit **Power** then **Restart**
2. The computer should restart and you'll be shown the screen for **Choose an option**
3. Choose **Troubleshoot**
4. Select **Advanced**
5. Then hit **Go back to the previous build.**

You may not find this option. In that case, simply follow the first method

System Restore

Another setting that we just can't seem to comprehend is Windows 10 choice to turn off System Restore. If you would like to turn it on,

1. Hit the **Start menu** and type in **Create a restore point**
2. This will open it up in the list and you just have to click it to open it
3. Select the system drive and choose the button to **Configure**
4. Enable **system protection**
5. Set the maximum disk space to be around 5GB. You may have to check this setting once in a while because recent updates may disable it automatically.

Printer compatibility

If your device is a little old, you might easily find yourself getting into problems with connecting to a printer. If you just upgraded from Windows XP or Windows 7 to Windows 10, you will first have to update the printer drives. When you do this, it will prevent malfunction after you update to Windows 10

This should not be difficult to do.
1. Enter into your favorite search engine and search for the printer's name.
2. Enter the producer's website and download the driver that'll be compatible with Windows 10
3. You want to make sure that you are not just downloading for a random website. Look for the website of the manufacturer.

4. Go through with the instructions given to you to install the driver and things should be fine.

Struggling with the touchpad

It's a good plus to have a laptop with touchpad and it should work fine with Windows 10. But some users have complained that the upgrade from an earlier Windows version makes it harder to use the touchpad.

The first thing you want to do when this happens is to turn on the touchpad. Some keyboards have a key that disables the touchpad so there's a chance you turned it on by mistake. If you don't have that key

- Move to **Devices**
- Choose **Mouse & Touchpad**
- Select **Additional Mouse Options**
- You will then see a new window. Select the **Device Settings** tab.
- Choose **Devices** and check to make sure that you turned on touchpad

If you go through these steps and you still face problems with your touchpad, you can try this
- Hit the combo; **Windows key + X**
- Choose the **Device Manager** option
- Hit **Mice and other pointing devices**
- Update the driver and things should start working fine

Needless notifications

The action center came in Windows 10 and it's simply a pane that collects the notifications on your computer so that you can sort things with them later on. A useful panel but it can become cluttered very fast because let's face it, not everyone has the time to addresses these unnecessary notifications.

You can filter out notifications that you know you wouldn't miss if they don't show
1. Enter the **Settings**
2. Move to **Notifications & Actions**
3. What you'll see now are different buttons for each app. Use these buttons to toggle an app.
4. You can also get to this place fast by searching for Notifications & Actions

10 Best Windows 10 Apps

Duolingo

Are you trying to improve your language skills? Are you hoping to go on a vacation to a country where they don't speak your native language? Do you think that a language class would help brush up your skills? Then Duolingo is the only thing you need to get you ready.

Duolingo is an app that allows you to learn different languages with tons of achievements and rewards for different quizzes that you pass. One of the reasons why we don't learn anything in language classes is because it's simply boring. But with Duolingo you are able to learn casually so you can sit and learn for a long time and you wouldn't even notice it.

The app wouldn't limit the number of languages you can learn at once. But even though learning 8 languages might sound like an incredible idea, you may want to limit your choice to about 2 so that you can keep a firm hold on the things you learn.

The user-friendly layout that Duolingo gives is what makes it one of the top choices for language learning. You also get to use the streak function which keeps you going by tracking how long you attained a goal. You can also preview more resources to hone your skills like Duolingo Stories. With this, you can find audio stories that give you a chance to check how well you can understand what is being said

Adobe Photoshop Express

While it true that not everybody can afford Adobe's full suite, nobody said you can't at least get a taste of what it is like to use Photoshop. You can easily download the free Photoshop version on your Windows 10 PC.

It is called 'Express' because you are able to use photo-editing tools from Photoshop but still do customized work. If you are familiar with Photoshop and would like to edit some photos, this app can be very useful. But when you get the app, you will need to use an Adobe ID login to start using the app, just something to keep in mind.

Adobe Photoshop Express wouldn't do everything that the Big guy can but it should be enough to make your pictures a bit more interesting.

Netflix

If you use mainly use your PC for more entertainment purposes than for productivity, then one great option is to download Netflix so that you can start using the app from your desktop. What even great is the fact that Netflix sync across your various devices.

What this means is that when you watch something on your PC and you leave for work, you can complete the movie or TV show on your smartphone while on the bus. You can also sync to your gaming consoles like Xbox.

But this doesn't mean that you can't watch Netflix until you download the app. If you wanted to watch Netflix media on your PC, you can easily fire up a browser that's compatible, Chrome is a wonderful option, and then you'll sign in to your Netflix account.

But going through that route has a huge drawback and it's the fact that you cannot download movies or TV shows on your computer to view offline. This is where the Netflix app comes to the rescue. With your computer on Windows 10, you can easily enter the Microsoft Store and download the Netflix app for free. Of course, you should have a Netflix account and a subscription to be able to enjoy movies.

Skype

When it comes to long-distance communication, Skype is still one of the most famous chat services and the best part is that it incorporates well with the Windows 10 OS. If you are already used to video chatting at work or home, you know the steps to download the service.

But for those who have not really video chatted before and would like to explore what a new communication service would be like with their family and friends, it doesn't get better than Skype so why not give it a chance.

There's a version of Skype that's already incorporated with Windows 10 but this official app will give you the option to share your screen, share photos or use translation.

Spotify

One convenient way to enjoy your playlists and tracks without disturbance is to listen to Spotify music on the Spotify app for Windows 10. You can easily get the original Spotify Windows app from the service's website, but you can also get it from the Microsoft Store since it has now been updated to the Windows 10 app we have today

Not only does this now make it easier to find, this modern app also brings some benefits of the Microsoft Store with it as you can download updates automatically and it will do so in the background without hassles. With this, you get to stay up-to-date

If you are looking to download the Spotify app on your Windows 10 PC through the Microsoft Store, here is a quick way to go about it

Fire up the **Microsoft Store**. If you don't know where to find it, you can start by hitting the **Start menu**. You will then see a tile showing you a white bag with the Windows logo on it. Select it.

When the Microsoft Store opens, enter in the name; **Spotify** in the search bar at the upper right corner of the page and search.

You should be presented with different apps that are related to what you searched. Find the green Spotify music tile and click that

This will then lead you to the Spotify music screen on the Microsoft Store app. Find the **Get** button so that you are able to download Spotify on Windows

This action should download and install Spotify on your computer and you would be notified when it's done and set to be used.

Dashlane

Many people try to cram all their 5,000 plus passwords into their brain hoping that they'll remember it when they need to login to the accounts of their bank, email and others. And the deal is that we all want our passwords to be secure.

Gone are the days of 1234, we now need a complex collection of numbers, characters and letters and you also need to find a way to remember them. Not everyone has a good memory to store passwords for different sites so what they just do is use the same password for all of their accounts.

You might think it's not a bad habit because no one can figure out your foolproof password but this is one of the biggest mistakes when it comes to using online services. Hackers can hack passwords and when they get one, they'll try it with a bunch of other accounts and see if it enters. And if that happens, your online identity would be a mess.

Some others try to write down their password traditionally. Yes, I know you're covering your eyes but a lot of people still do this. Let's forget about the fact that just about anybody can see those passwords, you also need to make sure you are with the journal every time so that you can write down and recall your passwords. But some try to use password managers like Dashlane.

Dashlane works by creating a secure vault to store passwords for users so that they can retrieve them easily when they need them. You can then lock all these passwords with one master password that you can set to anything you want. When you use this one master password, you'll be able to view the collection of passwords and usernames that you've stored with Dashlane.

The best part of this app is that it can work in the background so that when you try to sign in to a website, Dashlane will appear and provide login details for the site. You can select the preferred one. This is a much better option than you trying to remember and type in your passwords yourself.

VLC

Of the last couple of years, media players have greatly improved and if there's an app you should thank for that it would be VLC. It is an open source media player that quickly became a go-to app for many users. While the app specializes in video playing, it can also play audios and it's a wonderful app to have on your Windows 10 PC

If you have an Android or iOS device, VLC is also available on smartphones. One great thing about the app is the simple interface and you would quickly set it to be the default media player for your computer. It's also a great way to play a wide variety of video and audio formats – a feature not all apps have.

Malwarebytes

You have an antivirus software right? Well, whether you do or not, you may want to consider switching to Malwarebytes. There's a chance you would use the default Windows Defender which you automatically get with Win10 but it wouldn't be so bad to up your game a little

Malwarebytes has features that make it distinct. For one thing, it's free for the personal version and it is made to work manually. Simply download the app and run it once every week. You can run it more than that if you have your reasons.

The app can sense different kinds of malware and dangers and can also go around many programs. Even if your computer is already infected, it would still run. If you ever need help, the Malwarebytes forum is always there for assistance.

Another great thing about the app is that you don't need to wait for hours just to get a scan which is a huge plus. When most people think of malware protection, waiting for long periods of time immediately comes to mind. But the app provides Hyperscan which allows users to perform scans very quickly. And you can also multitask while Malwarebytes scans your PC

Dropbox

Chances are you are already using cloud storage but one cloud service that's taking the world by a storm is Dropbox. These days, it really isn't hard to find a service that would want to offer cloud storage for free.

By offering it to you for free, the plan is that you would have stored many things with them and you'll love them so much that you would pay to continue with them. Dropbox, on the other hand, doesn't give you a bountiful supply of free storage. If you are using the free plan, you get 2GB for personal use.

But one good thing about the service is that it connects well with your PC and works fine with file managers. It also gives you reliable security, integration with Office, ease of operation and many other features. Google Drive is great but space can get full very quickly by attachments saved in Gmail.

If you are looking for a great Dropbox alternative, it doesn't get better than Google Drive.

Affinity Photo

When Affinity apps started, they were only for Macs. But now, you can also get their apps on Windows and the Affinity Photo application seems to be making a name for itself.

If there's anything leading people to the app it's its low cost and the fact that you don't have to use it on a subscription basis. It shouldn't take long to install the app and users have reported a seamless and fast installation. When you arrive at the interface, it wouldn't take long to recognize it.

It definitely has the unique Photoshop look which isn't a bad thing because making a completely different interface wouldn't do much good for those looking for a Photoshop alternative - And this means everyone.

You still get the tools for adjustment and photo manipulation. Of course, they'll be in different locations and would take some getting used to. It also doesn't do much help that they are labeled differently. Like you may want to use the Healing brush as we know it in Photoshop but when you try to find it in Affinity, you don't see it. What you get is Inpainting which basically does the same thing.

About The Author

Trey Roland is has been an active tech researcher for some seven years. His **how-to** guides can be found on reputable tech blogs. He lives with his wife in a small house in Massachusetts.

Disclaimers

In as much as the author believes beginners will find this book helpful in learning how to use a Windows 10 operating device, it is only a small book. It should not be relied upon solely for all Windows 10 tricks and troubleshooting.

Made in the USA
Middletown, DE
22 October 2024